DAVANTE ADAMS

BY ELLIOTT SMITH

T0010010

Apex is distributed by North Star Editions:
sales@northstareditions.com | 888-417-0195

Produced for Apex by Red Line Editorial.

Photographs ©: David Becker/AP Images, cover; Ryan Kang/AP Images, 1, 26; Paul Spinelli/AP Images, 4–5; Joe Robbins/AP Images, 6; Shutterstock Images, 7, 10–11, 18, 19, 27; AJ Mast/AP Images, 8; Damon Tarver/Cal Sport Media/AP Images, 13, 14; Ben Liebenberg/AP Images, 16–17; Mike Roemer/AP Images, 20–21, 29; Nam Y. Huh/AP Images, 22–23; Todd Rosenberg/AP Images, 24–25

Library of Congress Control Number: 2022922221

ISBN
978-1-63738-551-7 (hardcover)
978-1-63738-605-7 (paperback)
978-1-63738-709-2 (ebook pdf)
978-1-63738-659-0 (hosted ebook)

Printed in the United States of America
Mankato, MN
082023

NOTE TO PARENTS AND EDUCATORS

Apex books are designed to build literacy skills in striving readers. Exciting, high-interest content attracts and holds readers' attention. The text is carefully leveled to allow students to achieve success quickly. Additional features, such as bolded glossary words for difficult terms, help build comprehension.

TABLE OF CONTENTS

CHAPTER 1

BiG PLAY

The Green Bay Packers line up against the Cincinnati Bengals. It's the fourth quarter. The Packers need to hold on to the lead.

The Green Bay Packers played the Cincinnati Bengals on October 10, 2021.

Davante Adams starts to run past a Bengals defender.

Davante Adams gets ready to run. His team's quarterback, Aaron Rodgers, starts the play. Adams sprints down the field. Two Bengals **defenders** are right behind him.

ALL-AROUND PLAYER

Adams is one of the best all-around receivers in the NFL. He can dart and swerve to get open for short passes. He also has great hands to catch tricky long passes.

Many football players wear gloves. Gloves make it easier to hold on to the ball.

Adams looks over his shoulder. Rodgers throws the ball. Adams reaches out and grabs it out of the air. It's a 59-yard play!

FAST FACT

Adams had 206 receiving yards against the Bengals. That was a career high.

Adams plays wide receiver. It's his job to catch the quarterback's passes.

CHAPTER 2

EARLY LIFE

Davante Adams grew up in Northern California. He didn't join the football team until his third year of high school. In his fourth year, the team won the state **championship**.

Adams went to high school in the city of Palo Alto, California.

In college, Adams played for Fresno State University. He quickly became a star. He scored 14 touchdowns in 2012.

FAST FRIENDS

Adams met quarterback Derek Carr in college. They became great partners. Adams caught many touchdown passes from Carr. One catch helped Fresno State win a **conference** championship.

Adams attended Fresno State from 2011 to 2013.

Adams had 131 catches and 24 touchdowns in 2013. It was the most touchdown catches of any player in college football that season.

FAST FACT

Adams wore the number 15 in college. Fresno State **retired** this number in 2022.

Adams runs toward the end zone during a game against San José State.

15

CHAPTER 3

GOING PRO

Adams played at Fresno State for two seasons. Then he decided to go pro. The Green Bay Packers chose him in the second round of the NFL **Draft**.

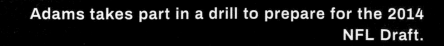
Adams takes part in a drill to prepare for the 2014 NFL Draft.

The Packers play at Lambeau Field in Green Bay, Wisconsin.

At first, Adams struggled. He made lots of mistakes. But he worked hard in practice. He also studied the game. He learned how to get open.

PERFECT PARTNERS

Adams joined quarterback Aaron Rodgers in Green Bay. They made a good team. Rodgers was very accurate. He always threw the ball right where Adams could catch it.

Aaron Rodgers (12) lines up for the Packers.

Adams catches a touchdown pass during a 2016 game against the Seattle Seahawks.

Adams's hard work paid off. He began to make more catches. By 2016, he was one of Aaron Rodgers's favorite targets.

FAST FACT

Adams had 75 catches and 12 touchdowns in 2016.

CHAPTER 4

STAR RECEIVER

Adams became one of the best players in the NFL. Between 2017 and 2022, he was named to six straight **Pro Bowls**.

Adams had 1,386 receiving yards and 13 touchdowns during the 2018 season.

Adams helped the Packers win many games. They made the **playoffs** several times. But they never reached the Super Bowl.

Adams helped the Packers reach the playoffs six times from 2014 to 2021.

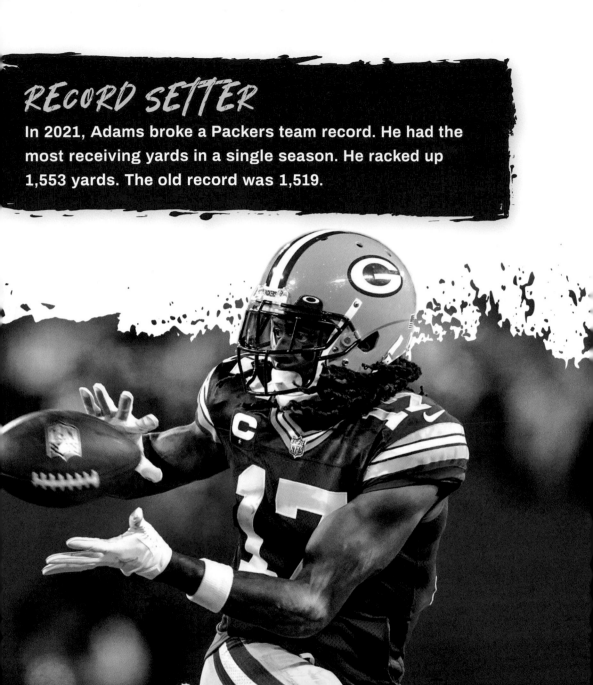

RECORD SETTER

In 2021, Adams broke a Packers team record. He had the most receiving yards in a single season. He racked up 1,553 yards. The old record was 1,519.

Adams scored 14 touchdowns during his first season with the Raiders.

The Packers traded Adams to the Las Vegas Raiders in 2022. He joined his old teammate, Derek Carr. They teamed up for many great plays that season.

The Raiders picked Derek Carr in the second round of the 2014 draft.

COMPREHENSION QUESTIONS

Write your answers on a separate piece of paper.

1. Write a few sentences describing the main ideas of Chapter 3.

2. Adams struggled during his first years in the NFL. But he studied and worked hard. What do you do when you face challenges?

3. Which quarterback did Adams play with in college?

    A. Aaron Rodgers

    B. Joe Burrow

    C. Derek Carr

4. Why did Adams become Aaron Rodgers's favorite target?

    A. He was a slow runner.

    B. He became a skilled catcher.

    C. He stayed on just one side of the field.

5. What does **accurate** mean in this book?

*Rodgers was very **accurate**. He always threw the ball right where Adams could catch it.*

    A. good at aiming
    B. stronger than most people
    C. good at reading

6. What does **partners** mean in this book?

*They became great **partners**. Adams caught many touchdown passes from Carr.*

    A. people who can't throw
    B. people who work together
    C. players on different teams

Answer key on page 32.

GLOSSARY

championship
A contest that decides a winner.

conference
A smaller group of teams within a sports league.

defenders
Players who try to stop the other team from scoring.

draft
A system where professional teams choose new players.

playoffs
A set of games played after the regular season to decide which team will be the champion.

Pro Bowls
Games played after each NFL season involving the best players from each team.

receiving yards
The number of yards gained by a receiver on a passing play.

retired
Stopped using a number on jerseys as a way to honor a player who used that number.

TO LEARN MORE

BOOKS

Coleman, Ted. *Green Bay Packers All-Time Greats*. Mendota
  Heights, MN: Press Box Books, 2021.

Hunter, Tony. *Green Bay Packers*. Minneapolis: Abdo
  Publishing, 2020.

Ryan, Todd. *Las Vegas Raiders*. Minneapolis: Abdo
  Publishing, 2020.

ONLINE RESOURCES

Visit **www.apexeditions.com** to find links and resources
related to this title.

ABOUT THE AUTHOR

Elliott Smith lives in Falls Church, Virginia. He enjoys
watching movies, reading, and playing sports with his two
children. He has a large collection of Pittsburgh Steelers
memorabilia.

INDEX

ANSWER KEY:
1. Answers will vary; 2. Answers will vary; 3. C; 4. B; 5. A; 6. B